] Praise for

Quaran tine

MW00425076

Amid a global pandemic, the ceaseless wildfires of California, a political landscape of turmoil, Millicent Borges Accardi offers us a powerful collection of self-reckoning. In *Quarantine Highway*—Accardi's fifth collection—the poems utilize repetition to both ruminate on and interrogate self and society, questioning the meaning and purpose of what we most often take for granted: the euphoria of memory, a trip to the Dollar Store, the intimacy of another's touch, and the illusion of safety in what has proven to be an unsafe world where "death is sudden, cold or both." What this collection offers is all that we can ask for, pray for, beg for, or demand, a praxis of survival perhaps in these uncertain times: "the sweet ride to anywhere, carrying the never-ending, hard-won secret of searching for who [we are]."

—**Ángel García**, author of *Teeth Never Sleep*

"Love is not a currency, neither is it an assignment," we read in a poem in *Quarantine Highway* and are reminded of the ways of love and of survival. These poems are gems that glimmer with insight and truths, mostly about living under the specter of COVID with both fear and hope.

I love the poems in *Quarantine Highway*. Not just because the writing is crisp and fresh and makes me want to write like that, but more specifically because they tease, surprise, and play even as they deliver soulful and deep insights.

The wordsmith in me relishes poems like "It was my mother who taught me to fear" where "The irregular verbs of culture that brought / the family away from The Azores, to the promised / land of California, was, were been."

With an immigrant lens that defies and armed with a linguistic deftness that challenges, these poems grind against expectations and bust open the façade, the nuance, and go straight to the heart, to the mind, confronting our current realities, living with social distancing and face masks for protection and yet fearful and at the mercy of an invisible invader.

I learned so much from reading *Quarantine Highway!* The many poems that referenced other writers took me down the google rabbit hole to learn and read poets and writers not in my immediate environs like Jose Tolentino Mendoça, and Inês Fonseca Santos as well as others known and loved like Nuno Júdice.

What a treasure trove! Accardi hits all the right notes!

—Norma E. Cantú

In *Quarantine Highway*, Millicent Borges Accardi guides us through the contemplative instances we explore in the loneliest parts of the pandemic with moving imagery and reminders of how to cope and recreate ourselves. In these poems, we reflect on healing, grieve on a lost year, dream of wildfires, and "tooth it out" beyond our anxieties of being undone. We pray to the "temple of our tragedy" and dance alone with small moments of liberation. Like breaking bread and memorizing trees, Accardi's poems step past comets that blast loneliness and cracks in the sidewalk from our childhood in order to help us rediscover all the connections we've missed.

—Juan J. Morales

Quarantine Highway

FLOWERSONG
PRESS

by
Millicent Borges Accardi

FLOWERSONG
PRESS

The History of Quarantine

The practice of quarantine, as we know it, began during the 14th century in an effort to protect coastal cities from plague epidemics. Ships arriving in Venice from infected ports were required to sit at anchor for 40 days before landing. This practice, called quarantine, was derived from the Italian words *quaranta giorni* which mean 40 days.

—Centers for Disease Control

Acknowledgments

Grateful acknowledgment is extended to the following publications in which these poems (or acknowledgment previous versions) first appeared:

Acentos: "Unlearning America's languages" and "Come Angels! Come Beasts"

Across the Social Distances: poetry in the time of the virus: "To Miss the Shadow"

Anti-Heroin Chic: "Broken Pieces" and "Inside me, Waiting a Long Time"

Another Chicago Magazine: "Bread" and "We'll Come Down"

BigCityLit: "Among Grotesque Trees"

Book of Matches: "The Right Measure of their Agony"

Burrow Press Review: "Echoes of a Room without Furniture"

FlowerSong Press: Good Cop/Bad Cop: An Anthology: "Before She Consumes it," and "Differently, the Way Everything is Wrong"

Digging Through the Fat (Digging Press): "Where They'd Gone to See Leaves," (print poetry series), "Days I Walked Home from School," (web journal)

Ginosko Literary Journal: "Darkness we are Having," "Side by Side in Fragile," "And Admits"

Globalpoemic: "The Undoing, "For Truth would be from a Line"

Jerry Jazz Musician--Poetry reflecting the era of COVID, Black Lives Matter, and a heated political season: "We Count Steps, Sweep Soreness"

Lumiere Review: "It's Almost Dark"

Melbourne Culture Corner (AUS)*:* "Holy Waters Heal the Border Scar," and "With a Whip for a Tail"

Knights Library Magazine: "With Beaded Rosaries"

Oddball Magazine: "We Still are not Breathing"

One Hand Clapping: "After all, they are Ridiculous"

PANK Magazine: "Broken Pieces"

Pendemic Journal: "She can do what She has to do" and "Yes it's Difficult"

Poetry Salzburg Review 37: "They Belong Perhaps to Other Worlds"

Sheila Na Gig: "Drowning Lined in the Sand"

TAB: The Journal of Poetry & Poetics: "Green was the Silence"

The Stand (UK): "Broken Pieces"

What Rough Beast (reprint) *Indolent Books:* "We Still Are Not Breathing"

Special Acknowledgments

Special thanks to the National Endowment for the Arts, the California Arts Council; CantoMundo; Fulbright; Fundação Luso-American (in Portugal); the Corporation of Yaddo; Jentel; Fundación Valparaíso in Mojacar, Spain; the Foundation for Contemporary Arts - FCA Emergency Grants COVID-19 Fund 2.0 and Barbara Deming Foundation, "Money for Women" for their generous support and encouragement.

TABLE OF CONTENTS

Quarantine Highway

Broken Pieces

All was if and maybe and meanwhile. The chorus
sang full of weed, a reflection on the acoustics
in the church, and--when does it ever seem all right--
When will that be again? The empirical
wish of a stupid requirement for happiness. Was that
what it was? And, they lived happily ever after is the phrase
perhaps you were looking for, a timid cool minute inside
your head when you used to believe otherwise, back in the slow
when time when it was not the new normal and, man,
it is not just us; it is global and inflated and then you know
it is terrifying, Did they take a census this year? 2020.
America, I seem to remember ten years ago
the government wanted to know our household income,
and what we did for a living.
This year? The form was all about age and race
and you could fill in whatever "other" you wanted.
Like a weakness, a mere description of how it was not
supposed to be.

To Miss the Shadow

It was a dare and a spit and a hope
that we were moving towards
a place, like chasing a storm
or running through a batch of luck.
No breathing out in the alley
like the tall grass they used to cut back
in the olden days when neighbors
talked over the fence at each other.
And, it was OK with God to like family.
Cause we were when and where and we
were how to in the outdoors where
we ran free. The future was all of a piece to keep,
a place to save us from. We were fearful
then of real things that meant something
to us, and it was in our power just to keep
silent in a grand fog of yelling voices,
trying to hold it all together even when it
was so not all right, and the doors were slamming.
Back in the day, we were all so self-important
and wondering-dreamy about ourselves.
And, we were sore and solemn, clueless,
like, like yeah it was impossible. Do you
remember that time when we held everything
in our arms tightly, as if we knew what we were talking about.

Bread

For those of us who know, knew
know, known, it was a bet that we made,
hoping for a last breaking of luck
before the world ran out.
It was betting and binding and--
I tell you--we were bleeding
as we went out to get cardboard
boxes in the rain and washed
over our souls with Clorox.
It was flinging a flung
while we tried to fly again.
To break bread, crusty and warm.
And, then life was forbidden and
everyone was an enemy.
The air was poison and spit was
evaporating into a daily forecast.
We were television-glued
as news rolled by and the rooms
misled us into doing the nonsense
we knew we shouldn't:
over-drinking, board games,
chanting curses at each other.
It was raining for three days
as I recall and the boxes delivered
on the porch got wet. I went
out there wrapped in bandanas,
with sanitizer and hope.
It was all there was and all we had
to stockpile with kale and bok choy
just in case. Of what?
The unseen war criminal that spreads

its over-washed hands wide across countries.
We want to leave, lose
lend, lie. We are shook and shaken
and looking for fever. For signs.
and it is all entirely unmanageable.

Side by Side in Fragile

Locate a crudeness,
a thought about
a fortress where help
is a sign of rumored comfort
and abandonment
means insanity, a lost
hope of what things used
to be, before the malice
set in and took over like
a new pleasure that used to
be painful. How can we do this
over and over without learning
from the missteps we make.
It's a sign in the back of
our heads, a cold-seeking
war machine that looks out for
where we are most damaged and
seeks the parts where we are
most awake and inside the most insincere and all weak-kneed
about, as we are hopeful,
It takes that away by
dodging reality and expecting everyday
to be an occasion, like Holy Ghost festas in June.
Home, the place where
we are drawn out and vulnerable because of
our dreams and the bounds of excess
joy we exude. The machine seeks out
where it knows we are in pain,
and can be cut off into that deep
hurt-contentment that no one ever
could fear or listen to or react towards.

Yes, far away from here, all the way
back to that back of the back-time when
everyone on your block was still
close at hand. That is where the machine sends us.

They Belong Perhaps to Other Worlds

from a line by José Tolentino Mendonça

Seeing a new range in which to live,
we plead, we engage, we bow, we
know, we realize, as if wishing were a political cliché.

There is so much to enquire and consume.
We order from Good Eats and Door Dash,
and wipe off the plastic bags and cardboard,

Seeming like we were advocates for begging
how to differ
or comment on an opinion. To reflect, my god,

to vanish. We pray and we dream, to dominate,
born only to distinguish, our weird
worldly support system gone, all,
within six feet of
social distance and water droplets.

While I Count Like I Have Practiced

on a theme from "Poetry Anxiety Disorder," Raina Leon

We count on our resilience
or however we come back or pick up like
our feet and sticks, or when we bounce
back or jump back to safety,
how we act like in a resilience, how we can
back together forward, away from old adversity
How can we be strong and vibrant when
We are not. We are told to be tolerant,
more tolerable than how humans were
meant to be, we respond to jumping
back in line with alacrity, not stepping.
When scolded to respond within the lines
colorful with lines within the lines
we see the lines of our face, like marked
borders left over to the light, taken
over, given back to the land.

The Undoing

There is impersonalness
to our touch, working backwards
from intimacy into being
mis-associated strangers,
what activities not to do any more:
touching cold feet in bed
or putting a washcloth to my face.
Are these acceptable gestures
now that we are rewinding into
the opposite of lovers.
We have tried to face the wall
inside the tunnel that is where
we used to travel through on our
way to being together, and we have pressed
in a non-onward direction,
like switching from left to right,
forced to hold the wrong hand,
to relearn how not to. How not to throw
and catch awkwardly. How to face
with the other shoulder, how to bend
the wrong way into a triangle,
into a new limiting direction
that keeps you trapped and strangled
and lost. Everything from scratch
transforming into a scar,
the places when you used to know
things by heart. Time is putting on
your right shoe and steadying
yourself on the left, jumping
around to keep a sort of balance
in an irregular circular way

--as if you are fooling yourself safe,
back on the ground and can protect
the country from falling, becoming
a universal key positioned into
the lock of how new life has become
unremarkable, disappeared and a lot more ugly.

For Truth would be from a Line

Inspired by Gastão Cruz

And, I would go, really.
And, is it about time we all got along,
but that was a no and the real answer would require
more sense than the crazy crisis
we are going through presently,
and the truth, ah. It would have to
be from a line
we used to know, an old phrase,
like a poem dealing with
trees I memorized, along with everyone
else in Mrs. Virtue's first grade
at Luther Burbank,
where the teacher handed out
pastel marshmallows
when we behaved.
For truth would have
to be untouchable,
like a hand we used to know,
to hold--
as if it were our own—
the left reaching
for the right, fumbling along thru
this magnificent universe we kind of
know, or at least pretended it to be so.

We Still are not Breathing

from a line by Alexis Smithers

And, we expect the temple of our
tragedy to disclose a first-hand
account of what is going on, that
little voice inside our head that says
murder, unfair and break down the ice.
Get through enough to talk back and say
all you imagine before the voice tells
you to stop all you wanted to do and be
and have and what has not happened
yet. It was as if we are at a café enjoying
brandy in a short glass and the clouds
build up in front of where we are sitting
And we consider loss in this
scene right before things all went down and happened.
It was what we thought of first before we
did not know any better, an attic of grief
and a piano that passers-by used to play
in the courtyard in front of the café,
and please, yes, I would like a basket of bread,
and some cold butter shaped into a square
rose. Love is not a currency, neither is it an assignment.
People are supposed to be born, knowing
how to love, no one learns how to kiss of course
they might practice on a mirror or with other
children, opening and laughing together
playing at being adults. Break the ice, as if you are
stopping a social stiffness. How can you not know
how to break through and touch me? Isn't love
like drinking water for thirst or words that
resemble gold. I am down for the count here.

Give me the bread and nod as the brandy sits
in its glass, in your hands, as they are holding it gently
like something that looks to be defeated, or nearly so.

Before She Consumes it

In somedark cases, or not at all.
This is what is happening
because we have all
done a job like this,
been at a party with someone's
brother-in-law who wants a kiss
by the kitchen sink all sloppy and talking
his game in a bag like nobody ever has done
that, and that is what is happening.
Because we have all done a job like
this, like nobody who has ever
done a job. As of this morning,
the top shelf dread was exceptional
and very valuable, a life un-reachable,
meaning to me, exceptional, like a strong
argument against an obvious problem,
like every day motions, where there is an elephant
in the corner or an obvious problem
we fail to address about what is on our mind
and the most important issue shoved to the
bottom of the sock drawer, against mis-matched
fragments and handkerchiefs, saved
since 3rd grade. It is what it is,
a room meaning how to ignore a large
failing problem, an issue that stands
out in a dangerous way, as if you are afraid
to cross the street or cannot speak your mind
Rather, it is that the world is ignorant,
a flat tool nobody uses, and you are an object,
something that looks delicious but is not exactly
mouth-watering when you bite into it,

a senseless, cannot stand the heat woman,
around for one night only, unable to cope
when with a guy who says No, I mean it, no
without gunning the car for a jump or asking why.

It's Almost Dark

And yet we remain inside,
as if living were a treat,
to walk around the block
unfettered is an adventure
not worth pursuing,
a blast for the words we
speak to scatter particles sparsely
into the air as our outer shells
harden and intensify.
We are here! It's a party!
Almost as if we do not know
each other's names anymore,
like the years we knew
outside confinement had
mushroomed away
Like a stark vision on the horizon
as we watch the sun go down.
As if to say, "Hey let this pass us by."
Like a spark or a soft punch hit
to the gut, we are conjoined
in spite of ourselves, queer and clueless
as we approach the rim of loyalty, together
in a small space, our pairing off is a reason to advertise
our faith and contempt.

As Among Grotesque Trees

We amuse ourselves through the absurd
April forest, comical and childish,
dupes in this quarantine of looking
for breadcrumbs, a pathway out.
Set aside on a fool's errand, seven times
funny and infantile, the dance of
the woods creating stockpiles of leaves,
like court hesitators we wash tree bark
And dance together, alone,
gullible and lighthearted. We pretend
this is an elongated day or game of Heads Up 7-up,
a cycle of twenty four hours of mockery
and nonsense. A fool's errand.
We are practical jokers,
pickling radishes and purple cabbage, steeping apple
cider vinegar in warm water.
We watch too much bad television like Tiger King
and Love is Blind. Tomfoolery abounds and we
yell Rabbit, Rabbit when we wake
up in the morning, the cause of everything.

The Right Measure of their Agony

Was cross-stitched into an under-belly
of a soul no one prayed to.
The right measure of their agony
endured and singled out the agony
as to what to do and think and be real
about, even when living was impossible,
to expose and enjoy and MAN it was
what just we were feeling in the moment.
We were all about the Woolworths
on the corner and making a film
with Super 8 on the roof of the apartment
where we smoked pot and talked
about AIDS and deconstruction. It was
the cozy nest we ran away to, to get divorced,
and where we pulled out the bed from the wall to fuck on.
As if it were the last time. We held spiders
and drank home-brewed absinthe as if we
were characters in 1920's Hemingway. We agreed
to the word double-life as we ventured on the fire escape
and we were solid, unbreakable and under the age of 30,
with that unfinished feeling that troubled us,
like not knowing your lucky number.

And Admits

In heart-felt kind
That things were flat
That it had been a many
Too long day of this day's solitude
And when we at thought we had it all
And life was just starting
And just starting it was like that for
More than half a lifetime
Like that when the riches
of being busy and flush full of normalcy
were clearly outlined
as honest as perfect timing
when a rabbit jumped
away from a hawk.
We were rolling down the street
Listening to Beethoven
And drumming the side of the open
Window with our feet
Hanging outside
As we turned through the fields of
Almond groves stupidly
being, almost whole
the subtle trunks thick and solid
awaiting years of height,
Subjected to grief, sadness
And a slick flush of wet jealousy
We ran afoul of the flames
That we were running towards.

We'll Come Down Close Behind

And such and we have
and we need and we want
and we have and if it happens,
we couldn't leave, and there is not a
never in the universe except now.
And but and and and for and if
Our place to live, it is a song
let it run peacefully into
the coda or the second chorus
where the refrain takes over.
And such and such and the homeless,
and prisons, and why can't I
leave my home without a mask.
We'd come down close behind
In the middle of a crowd, as if we
mattered and as if things were
normal rather than a new normal,
which is odious. Then, then and then
and could. Once, existence was on
full speed, catching rumors,
and touching faces and going outside.

Yes it's Difficult

from a line by Inês Fonseca Santos

And so the tirade extends like a chemical
mixture in an extruder.
It pushes and pulls back until the tail end
of the hurt is knifed off and another section
is extruded. After that, and then after that,
more after that's, and the bulk of it is all bullshit.
We were once invincible and carefree,
able to walk the streets, ride busses and talk to each
other as close as if to kiss and kiss we did, with tongues
and teeth and then as a hello we kissed each other's
cheeks on opposite sides, saying, "Yes I am with you"
and "We are the same." But it was all so easy
then, and it was how we did things then,
dirty and up close and we breathed on each other
sighing air, sipping in fine water droplets
into each other's lungs. As kids we ran over
to the Yannis family to catch chicken pox,
and leaned out the window to hug mom
When she got the mumps at 40. It was simple and sweet
and maybe how life was meant to be when we held up our
wrists, someone came to pick us up and whisper hush.

Let your Eyes Slide over the Estuary

from a line by Nuno Júdice

Man, it is as if we are cotton. Like in a wonderland
of what if and then there is another time
and we are lost. I don't know how long
this will last since it has taken over
who we are so much so and then over
and otherwise. We always knew it would
be this way until at knife-point it wasn't.
The slip and the fall and turn of the screw
we face every day, I 'm like OH god can we
touch the cardboard or bring in the mail?
I find myself spraying Lysol on the paper
as if I mean, as if the fuck we don't
know. No one knows. How long does the virus
last on a surface? On marble or plastic.
How long does it survive? We leave
the cardboard on the porch and count
to 24, a magical number we believe in
somewhere else. We are running
out of Clorox wipes, a half a pack
left. I swear the universe is unsafe now
and we watch movies like comfort
and we are going solo like the greatest we
that we have ever been is inside
the moments that we do not understand any more.

She Can Do What She has to Do

Oh my. We spin and crap it. What, all
of it We spin, and I cannot say what it is
or who we are and now, what, hey,
what is this? We dance and
drink wine and consider the days when
it was all possible before it wasn't.
Like, hey and, wow, and I don't know
any more. There are no answers here.
I sit in a café that I know does not exist,
on a corner in make-believe Paris. Yeah. I know.
The waiter pours pastis from a tall
pitcher, and I watch people in the plaza
in front of me, and it is sunny and, thank you,
I would love a piece of cheese and some
bread. The drink is cool, so I feel as if
the story of my life can go on forever,
as if I can have a time to tell the family
back home that I made it to France,
to the novels I dreamed about like *Sun Also Rises*,
and—hello--I will walk to Hemingway's
in Montparnasse, with a nod to Hadley,
then sit on the horse-shoe barstool
at La Closerie. This is convoluted and stupid
and, yeah, but it is my whole world right now.
I could have been someone else entirely,
a checker at Safeway, which is not half-bad, and perhaps it would
have meant more to me then, but, and if, after,
I imagine myself. What if I not lost my New Bedford
accent, and the space between my teeth? What if I had
not assimilated into a new version of what
I thought I needed to be.

At Close of Day

My god. I am so sick of the phrase, at the end of the day.
Not Les Miz song, but when people say it
as punctuation or a reason as to why.
As if no one knows the conclusion as to
how things are now. Actually very few do or can plan the end.
Perhaps Ginsberg who had a Tibetan drummer
and beautiful boys carrying incense. Other than that,
death is sudden, cold or both. Like whammo.
No one cares, no one can predict. There are tons
of friends who hope you Get Well but every
few who hang in there through the years
of not getting better or getting worse, just skating
along being not OK and not OK, until it is suddenly
an emergency and then poof goes the world
as it opens up and cousins you have not
heard from for 40 years come out of the wood work
demanding a response, a presence, an answer to their
call to the nurses' station like MY GOD I AM HIS COUSIN.
As if all that builds power. I have been through that
evil and criminal and making someone sign a form
when their head is not right, so money can be
stolen, without knowing a person.
Man how is that possible in America?
And yet it IS. People you do not know
cozy up to parents and great aunts, whispering them
in their ears—like, Hey, I knew what you were when you were,
and they are afraid. We are all afraid. And it is wicked and awful
and there is nothing you can do except call up to the clouds of your
mother in heavenly heaven and say, Yes, at the end of the day,
it is what it is.

What we Call Time

In the such in the such
Of the such and such,
of different feels, we
are
in search of quarantine
days,
spraying cardboard with Lysol,
against the virus appearing
like a red, notched microscopic
yarn ball.
The enemy is agile, and
we cannot
touch metal or wash
our hands without
singing a
birthday song. We wish away
rights to handshakes, and
watch old
movies with longing,
where couples kiss
on the mouth, in the dipped shoreline
of Florida and hold onto each
other's necks.

Left with Loose Sentences

from a line by Margarida Ferra

The day has a hard shadow
he said, where the sun cuts
behind a solid object like
a resolution, or
a song the lady
reads aloud, like a story
about failure,
or a year's
loss into oblivion that
no one planned for,
the inability to get anything
done. Being lost without
redemption.
No joy, but solitude
found in penalties,
lost imaginings
and tasks, lost amid,
behind,
for what remains unfinished.
This day's long life, mapped
between reality
and denseness,
as bottomless as a break
in the dark house up inside my heart.

Decorate Fear

Decorate fear, desperate
for slow sliding down a hill
as if we are
turning up our lips in
a strained, extended snarl.

Decorate fear, desperate
fear, we think

all day of dancing
the Vira de Roda, faster,
front-to-front without holding hands.

The steps weighing us down
Like from the sap
from trees, sticky and often
brown,
we touch air, not hands
and step into the circle of
each other,

far away from who we are
Now. What we are named.
How the world is.

Faster and faster,
Now,
front-to-front without holding hands.

It Made her Feel Like

She could stop
the whim of the whistle-blowers,
easing her out of her life and into
the dread. It was hours after an afternoon,
or, maybe, Thursday. Does it feel
like more like a week ago.
Or, is it lost like a decade and--oh my goodness--where
did the scissors disappear to. A few breaths away
it was 1992 and the world seemed to
spin on my axis, in downtown Loose Angeles,
where I was silly and things were once cared about,
a gypsy dress from the Boardwalk before a party
was toted out to look at and smile.
A missed phone call to come into work.
A friend yelling at me upstairs.
In 2020, I cannot imagine driving
on the freeway or waiting in line.
Everyday things slip through my slipping place
And my fingers, close and easy as sodded
dirt, now, and I focus on things
at hand, that I can reach for,
tasks obtained safely, close to from where I am
sitting. It is the darkness
that tells me what to do,
or the awful, for it is my time that tells me
to be the opposite of night
and the walls chewing into the walls.

Differently, the Way Everything is Wrong

from a line by Kim Göransson

And we sing-song through our days,
like everyone who was last changed,
going finally and patiently cold,

as if we were passing
across a reservoir in the water still
and cold, like, as if you had said yes,
as if we had always quietly, nervously,
bravely, beautifully said those things

that we knew, that by best I would have known
and which your words would have won me over
in a second if I had not stopped to think
about it.

There was a common bang and crash
between us, and we were a comedy
troupe at the door of a silent movie,
in the dog-dead lies of every open Friday.

Everything worthy of extreme and easy
The words that we thought up enough
about, for and of that but it should be easy
firstly, this courtship, and ever-urgently
we ran into love and fun-forever
we fell.

We were great and nearly as fun
as if we had all imagined
what life would be about if and when

we were trying to understand
the impossible-immediate that
we realized who we were meant to be.

The notion of do not forgive at any cost
was lost on us, those who dreamed of
the impossible alley-way,
the instead, the immediate.

It was all we wanted.
This is what we knew best.

Inside me Waiting a Long Time

from a line by Rusty Morrison

We were off to the races,
hope and madness, lost
compartments of helplessness
where my wrist are pins and needles
and I cannot think of where to look next,
the body yelling back and forth like
A see-saw in a playground,
where someone keeps jumping
on and laughing, high in the air, screaming.

It was push pull and out of sorts,
That I find myself explaining
Justifying and unliving memories
to someone I saw 3 times in the past
20 years. This is how it is now, these days

in which we are like summer bugs,
trapped in a screen door.

Reinforce this anger of anxiety,
filled with no more conversations. Everything
Is a moral code. The day fills with

predators, trying to find weaknesses,
a bet, a metal slide, the rocket into a pile of sand.

We are free and we
and we are cutting through our thick distance
like youth.

The World can Turn Upside Down

Speech, beg, delay.
You do what I hate
most about me. How can it be,
that the things
that stop me from controlling my own
starship
are what you throw down
as a roadblock to my
star field, my entry point to Orion's belt.
This is not the last mention
of what we had
to do. It was only one thing
to keep straight.
That was all.
It was supposed to take five minutes
to justify
How it was gonna be, and we are all over
the point of checking out
the comet as it blasts thru our earth times
of loneliness.
Once. there was time and a spare
when both of us forgot
to mention the delay.

With me, you can feel like a Horse Race

I said to no one in particular,
cause every day at all times, over and, yes,
there are people waiting,
perpetually, who are throughout all time
in one place, continually saying
"God is always the same."

During a certain period,
at a regularly at stated interval,
the gears shift and bellow.
They are invariably, uniformly, ready
for anything to be thrown at them.

You see, you need to press the words
she said, folding her gloves
in her lap as if she were from
another time.

In any event, the day was
Good, good, and entitled and yet still serene
and beautiful. Money,
we could see it in the future
closeted and held for us
to take back like a treasure
when this is all over.

In the bleachers, we were white,
abysmal and vast, on display,
in full plumage of our shabby selves,
wrapped around a life we could
only imagine of in vain.

As if we had never happened at all,
and what was left behind
was sordid and cheaply in limbo.

We are plausible, primitive, vast
and unseemly, solid
in our step and solid to push away
from ourselves. We are easy to follow.

Static in place like a strange, blind
unpacked moment we stand
waiting for the next race to begin.

Flat and yellow like cloth,
the earth kicks up when the horses
start at the gate.

And, we need needles for
sewing our souls behind
into a dress that is sunny and would

have changed the wonderful and
the infinite wrong of this day into

a beautiful sun-baked moment of bliss.
There is an ordering to our days, now,
trapped, in and out of order.

Too late. I was Already

from a line by Marilyn Kallet

He said, "My behavior was inexcusable,"
and it ended like a dull thump
of softness. The fields I had run
through like a scenario were useless,
as were my arguments and counters
to a distant cousin who was arrogant and unimportant,
a bully not meant to be taken
seriously until you are trapped in the moment of
a middle and of whatever is going on, and then
you fight back without thinking or
taking a pause. How dare he. How come.
Why on earth, highlighting every weakness
by taking and spinning takes. The hurt
torn open and thrown apart inside, to reappear
in an image of only the same person
you were ten minutes ago, bound
up into a ball in the corner, looking proud,
solid, and sentimental, glued to a city
where you no longer live, too close to rage
aloud that you do not care. In fact you do too damn much
for the hurt to be real. Swing. Remain. Nightmare.
Turn over the table in front of you.
Everything possible that can be done is brought
forward, half gone and already too late.

I Swear, Don't

Was it something that happened,
or was there ever a time when things at least seemed
OK. What was it inside us that happened
when we lost all of our luck
stripped away down to the threads.
The un-luck went from one
to another like
touching your face and being afraid.
We were there and then, and it was
not all right way too soon to tell and, yet,
it is what is happening now.
We are here and we are sorting
things out and staying
home. No matter what we find there
in the boxes or drawers, make no mistakes
here my friend, we are afraid,
of boxes and cardboard and breath.
We grow anxious when someone
comes to the door. When the phone rings
or a branch breaks off in the wind
and cracks on the deck wood as it falls.
It has been years this time.
And, now, only the rest of the
world is setting out their own table
of fear, plates on linen, sharp knives
fear, which is just like our own.

The Past Recent Times

That I cannot hang up on getting
a turn which way wherever something
goes like a bumper car, my days
are jostled, and all I can do is push
through into plugging my ears.
How can I tell. I crawl through
agonizing over decisions that used
to be easy and twist-turn into
problems I have been over
stating and preparing for in a distinctly
out of touch way. How can words
resonate. How can I tell. Thinking
things through the order and selection
of our species is a new madness.
A madness of the first degree
With which to reach only
a mistake before I even take a damn
step outside. This is a resolution
I ask myself not to ask.
How do I know what I used to be.

In Oblivion

It is as if the world's engines
have ground to frozen metal in the middle of
the midst inside a clutter clutch

of busy confusion and everyone
has been cast off, from the
blissful-working-gears we used
to down shift into.

Those pointless mental locations
where we find ourselves fretting
about things that cannot be repaired.
We drift in this new future

in the now of the stopped moment
of where we are as we are being
lost now, again, inside out and stuck
in deep stagnancy,

We are adrift and paralyzed, both,
making do with what we have laid out
before us, stretched apart like a knitted
cloth.

We are ambiguous, a lost
part of speech, left behind.

In Later Time

We were handsomely accessible
during that period of cocooning, all warm
and quirky, decisive and boring,
learning new ballads of how to be
flippant with each other. There was
violence in the air, and I kept asking
myself what is another word for suffuse?
Continuing to move about, deep in a terrain
of the swampy mud of foggy minds,
we were inattentive and distracted,
speaking to each other while jumping back and forth
between the bed and couch. Asking questions
as if we did not anticipate any response.
The white walls growing yellow,
a vacant-distant form of age, like our skin, marshy
and shattered. We were dull, and full
of no one but ourselves when we tried
to concentrate in the pandemic, but misplaced
thoughts that grew muddy, directed us that
our thinking was off as if we had woken
from a lie-in and then lost one another.
Like my mother used to say, We were dull
as dishwater. As if to say, we were filthy, fat and
unmoving, except to stir when the outside got dark,
when the inside was a long smash of heavy,
dense, thickness, like a labyrinth we could not tear
ourselves out of or away from.

Caught Fire, with Fire

This is no time for hope.
It is a time for prediction as to
what comes after. When you must
listen to what others say about you
and ignore it. Like a squeaky joint
or a ball of pain inside your forehead
that cries: Stay, safe, remain. It is all
what it says it was. As if air had been raised
up into a dangerous place where no one can
live, above the atmosphere that sustains life,
all we can do is pace the floor
and remedy ourselves with survival
techniques and distractions. We never
knew it could be this way, and we object
to the upset of the influx of data and false
domination by the worded cage who shouts
from the pulpit. It was a mere objection
to what we most needed, the earth caught
on fire with fire, and we are trapped here.
Can we seek or explain? Is there like a sign
in London, called a Way Out?
Please explain, Gloria, has the cat
got your tongue? Are we offended
when we read between the lines.
When we push against dependence, the source of all we
Authorize. Where is the wonder? The leaks
are too much to overflow, and they work into the ancient
feeling of it as if it were it not a wonder at all
but life overwhelming, a solution we cannot solve.

Slowing Things Down

It Was
a
Careful
Damning
Bruise that
would otherwise be
looking like
a flame though
thickening glass,
dense as a planet.
A bruise
that made them fall

Where They'd Gone to see Leaves

from "Cue Lazarus" by Carl Marcum

Drawing a blank, meaning
the words leaving or leaves do not side up that
parallel universe any more unless
the truth is more than that, like,
it is a multiple choice test about
of which definition is closest to the
meaning, the essential failing
to recall a memory, falling into
another scene, or unable to retrieve
the name of a face I can know
and know and know. A lost baseball
over the neighbor's fence.
Unable to remember a piece of cotton
hanging on the plastic line in the backyard
or why my mother's
voice was high-pitched that day when
we all found out. The opposite
of confinement, the not knowing is liberty
in a way, something new in an abyss
of starting over, to random
new cities. Always starting over.
Only then, we did not know it.
At one point in the future, I can only
imagine that I will have his name,
or know the way his green Buick Electra pulled
into the driveway on Cherry when he got home
after working at his shift at Sears.

After all, They are Ridiculous

A weigh-station, a border control office
without guards. They slink in
with gnawing and noises
deep in the floor wood.
Not hunting for food, they rush through
on their own time-tables.
A family or a solo one, it is hard to tell
when the noises shuffle through
the hours of our time
confined to the near air of our home,
away from the broadness of the weather,
a few feet from the closed back door.
We are anxious and glazed-over,
famished for human touch and bewildered
by the new shake of smoke outside,
the helicopters overhead circling
the canyon in search of fire. We hear sleep
and fear the time that we are learning to endure
with growing complacency. The logistics of making do
with an earnest belief in living, still. They arrive
at 5pm or with the orange rise of scheduled dawn.
As we are sitting up in bed, surrounded by
folded pillows, they crinkle paper below
the box spring and charge ahead for
where the doorways meet the
wall on the other side. We throw bottles
to the floor and swear at each other
that this is not right. But it is endurable,
and then we are charmed, and sit back,
feeling closely akin and locked into the
nearly god-loving sense of their wandering,

of being busy and wanting to feel comforted, even if just for a fleeting moment; the desire to belong temporarily even somewhere.

There's Always a Woman

"Ay Llorona" — from *Self-Portrait with Weeping Woman* by Deborah Paredez

Leaning against the bed,
near sex or death or anger,
she is playing for meaning,
praying for keeps and you know
and I know that this is about
to get serious. She says words
like love and freedom.
It's her dire talent for always
being good in difficult situations,
and being easy when it counts.
Like I said, things are about to get
serious. There is 48 hours
and labored breathing on a left side that stops
working. We are in communication
every few hours with the monster
in the new year that we cannot speak
of, the laughter on top of the euphoria we
touch for a little while, and then breathe out
droplets of words like time and wait and
how much longer until we all grow distant.

All it Takes

Is advice that you follow by the book
And don't wallow in your subject
or substance, and you follow and listen
Keeping your mouth shut. You follow
the twenty ways that Mary tells you
to get rid of the ants in the kitchen.
You spray peppermint and douse lemon
On the tile counter as you roll out
a carpet of diaphanous earth
and a carpet of white Borax
as well as copper bands around
the tight cabinet drawer handles.
You drink cod liver oil and chant
Go home go home go home as the
ants pick up their dead and march
backwards to their queen.

Holy Waters Heal the Border Scar

from "Border Bullets" by Norma Cantu

Two babies sorted and taken from skin
like property. Stitched back into
the olden days
harshly across water from hip to hip,
in uneven edges, a scar torn open again
and again and made new
each time
the edges were torn, open ripped
and away, like land lost
or a life taken.
Falling down the banks, her children
disappeared when she was
laid out on her back,
spaced between on passages of the
sweat sheets for longer
than necessary.
It was economical and virtually complete
her journey from woman to possible
and then made equal
all was wide and lost into everything
all knowledge that was clear
and frank-necessary.
As if she were for now, both
boundless and brief,
like bullets.

But now our Nightmares are Tinted and Fulgent and Crackling like Neon—
from "Orange" by Carlo Matos

So now we know. And are presented with what to choose: the silver coffin,
or the basic copper. With linen or crepe And it is our way to
guide the wishes of the dead, to choose to honor even when
it seems hopeless. And personal religious beliefs, that's right,
virtually completed so much longer true-longer
than the greater good and further than we, we
ever thought we could deal with.
It is calling and paperwork and potentially
unpleasant things we have to approve
and say run together with granite inscriptions, embalming
and difficult relatives.
Each department separate like estranged
family members, wanting
control, to stop, to say they,
hell, they all lie when they say and stave off and beg and grovel and assert
and pretend to need time to gather
their thoughts cause the truth is
NO ONE follows through after they have put you
off on a stall tactic. Wrapped you away
in front of a Vegas sign on the strip
that says Circus Circus.
No one ever says, Hey it has been that hour
or that day that I said I needed
to sort through and dust off
my beliefs and what I was going to say.
Yeah. agora sempre.

Days I Walked Home from School

Was Bewitched reruns and kale soup,
cheaper than cafeteria food. A TV tray
set up already when I swirled in
after getting past the Junipero pervert and
running the alley. It was all scary,
pretending to be all right
and there were gangs and getting jumped
on your birthday, and I was bused to another
school after this one, where the other
girls had Sassoon jeans and Ann Taylor scarves.
The blue bus that brought me two hours
to junior high where there was a special
garden for the 9th graders, and candy
apples at nutrition. It was all that
I wanted and wanted to go skiing and
Hawaii, but, we got government cheese
from Weingart Center,
and Margo sewed my brown skirts
from industrial-made cloth
she got at Repp and Mott auction. It was that
way and the counselors told me that
I liked to read and there were libraries,
and I liked to read. I was the boldest
and most dangerous, sunny disposition I knew.
Every weekend rewriting *Little Women*
in a made up binder I put together
out of three rings held
together with paper and pink yarn.

With Beaded Rosaries Wrapped

from "Crooked Pinkie" by Celeste Guzmán Mendoza

Old Souls come and go in fits of sanity
and fortitude, we seek through
the inter-workings of planning
a service that was supposed to be
Ave Maria and seasons of floral
arrangements, a crowd honoring
a life lived well and then
there was corona and distance and
no one can be there or get through
the walls that have been built.
All we have left is a perhaps internment
With marble walls, locked gates
and special permits. Like the opposite
of a life celebrated and mourned.
Life, in her, but there is loss and limbo
and waiting. The eternal disappointment
of weariness and serenity. She had last rites.
She wore the outfit she had selected.
There is more to do nothing. The rosaries
are named by her grandchildren and they slip
through our water like fingers.

In the Sewer of my Soul

from "Night Sweats" by Ángel García

Oh man there is a whatever or a loss
and bottom of the pit of laughter and hate
we always wished things would have been
different and those strongholds
we held onto as a kid disappeared
when people started dying
No one warned or told you about that
 cause you always thought
it would be the same way with a dock ramp
of stability out there in the euphoria
of life, waiting for you, each next door
opening to a new way to be how things
were gonna work out better and only
bad people were the ones who were lost,
they who made bad decisions
and turned right in a moment of accidental
regret and you were never gonna be that.
Even though wild things are skimpy
and dicey and you are worried there was is
a solid sense of how things should
be and a sense of right and wrong up on top
of a bottom line, like the sand on the ground,
tracked in later. As you slide down
the metal elephant in the park for a mom
who is waiting for you. Maybe she had to ditch off
 to work and take a bus and three
transfers or maybe the mom was your neighbor
who had a signature card at your elementary,
saying it was OK to pick you up. Or grandmother,
but it is someone instead

that you could count on, sort of like floating
holidays or sleep, as sweet as warm milk,
or all of the things you used to count on being there.

Could it be that Maybe this Crazy Situation is the Reason

from a Tina Turner song, for Rosebud

I don't quite understand what is happening
or how to fix it, to come up with a travel
plan inside my blood, to worry out
a list of items to remain and those to
cast off, or give away to where they can
find their own sense of urgent history.
I hear the refrain, ""let the bodies of people pile high
for him"
All days are spent building a labyrinth
With shortish temptations and brick walls
at every turn. "let the bodies of people pile high
for him" We cannot simply bother
not to whisper any more. We rush into
the streets and on social media
to say no, and there must be a way
to fix this, to fuse what feels like two
life wires sparked with juice, how to join
them back together, if they ever were
back together or maybe even joining
the wires as we always knew it was the
right thing to do in the first place.

Drowning Lined in the Sand

It was a sign of discouragement
The outlined pattern near a castle
Left behind, like a utility line
Lingering on the ground without juice

We walked past Muscle Beach
That winter, the brilliance of the
Sun cut down by clouds, the durability
Of the boardwalk weathering
Change. The giant chess
Game, lined up before the
Ocean bleachers, a sign of
Redemption among the ruin

The fences erected to fight
Erosion, keep out the tourists
Too, fires burning the last
Synagogue and the house
Next door.

That year, the tents moved in
Taking out the street vendors
Hawking bags of rolled up
Socks and T-shirts three for
Twenty dollars, wrapped
And held into place with rubber bands.

On the side streets below
Lincoln, near Oakwood
Off Abbot Kinney, the trucks
And vans set up house

With buckets and taglines
Hooked into the electrical
Poles, bootlegged backyard
Hoses, stretched nearly
A block, warm bodies huddled
Together in insanity or honor
But never both, an offseason
glimpse of patriotic or what we have instead.

Echoes of a Room without Furniture.

from "Dead Dead Darlings" by Carolina Ebeid

What type of word is freedom.
That opposite of cluttered, fettered, alone in the world.
Is freedom unlimited or open,
meaning beyond the imaginary beautiful slate
of clean. Is it perfect, describable,
something to be defined, refined and designated,
an empty room to fill up with stuff made of glorious
new, conceptual, inadvertently unattached objects. The end
of lost and the beginning of found. It is unlimited
and open, calm and unimaginable. How have you walked
past Beverly Manor and not waved at the seniors
in the common area. Describing how
freedom feels can be unmethodical and calculated.
Am I the same person as you. Are we all gathered here
for a purpose of which is also unlimited or static,
a handmade sign that reads, "Continue Now."
A soul held precious by a specific value point
we all reach at least once in our lifetime,
when we get it that there is no one else to count
on, on less than one hand--except ourselves--and we know it,
and it is said that the opposite of impossible is
grounded and settling, an anchor we drop.
And we all know childhood is over when we know the truth.
It is what it is not. Life is not what you make of it.
But, what is dished out to you, and how you manage
along despite yourself, talking narrow and straight
on a verbal path, yet hoping that it will all work out.
Let's pretend it is Christmas, and we get to relive
every day in anticipation and with a little death inside us
hiding under the floorboards, where, the luck will return

to save us, to make things right as the rain we always knew
the story of, the wonder that we knew would straighten itself
out for long enough to be real, and you get reach up your hand to be held
by Mom when you visit Aunt Anna in her room with a pull
down bed, and she hands you orange butterscotch
that sticks to the candy dish with the wrapping left there.

With a Whip for a Tail

from "Tracing the Horse" by Diana Marie Delgado

The horse is not a party game; this is some real
skin and shit and animal. I meet him on the trail,
taller than me, and feel his ribs moving under
my legs and I am found. For the rest of the Wyoming
summer, I am out in the hay and comparable
ranch weeds, tied to the rough rope with the others
on a trail, bumping through chores, sorting
out and bending over under tree limbs
and assorted rocks. I even try to make friends
with the girls on the next cabin from Oregon,
who wear braids with blue bows that their mom puts in,
every morning. I am found and philosophical,
and then I repeat my words from a high saddle
above where the ground used to be.
I cannot hear the trail blazer or the cowhands
cause this land is family, and I am down for the
count, to face the fires at night. We cook meat
over red coals in the ground, and there are above
stars, where I can see inside the outside of the dark
moon, and we know we want it all.
We want to take things on and ride them
along, into the ground, unfettered and bitter,
all of our troubles becoming a complete transformation
beyond the city we knew, Ha, it is absolute, my confidence
and with my moss boots that I bought with pennies I earned
babysitting. I know how it is. How to cook a fried egg
in sizzling butter until it browns and makes a crust.
I know how to feed the fire in pit with cotton wool.
The rest of things I see are repulsive and dangerous.
Distant to me now, cause I am on a sweet ride to anywhere,
carrying the never-ending, hard-won secret of searching.

Unlearning America's Languages

on a theme by, "Lowering Your Standards for Food Stamps" by Sheryl Luna

We spit and spill and sit on our hands,
trying not to react. We found philosophical absolution
in not knowing, feigning knowledge that ours was the generation
where we were form-fitted into a dress of forgetting
language culture, food, Fit in Fit in Fit in
disappear into America and all of its joys
and death threats because that is a white wall
of promise there it is in front of you my friend.
A wall to blend into and hope for the best.
Be public-charming and the opposite of deliberate,
un-thoughtful and loose. Let's wait quietly
before the others speak and never let on
the name of your street or where your family
came from and that was and is how it was.
Parents came to California to rise above while
blending inside a fairytale Knott's Berry Farm where
Old McDonald feeds the chickens and a city where
kids ride bikes and play Pong. It was sleep
and rise and keep damn quiet about anything
different. Tell the counselor you will ride the bus
and stave off the earthquakes, embracing a future
that does not resemble any past you heard whispered
and fought about at night after bedtime, where
we lie in bed and draw words in the air, spelling
out where we came from.

With Cascading, Iron Straight Hair

from "Heirlooms" by Luivette Resto

Slathering on lye from an orange jar with a hopeful
grin. The fumes going straight to my nose.
I use lye like hair conditioner, wanting wings.
like the other 70's girls, who can brush
and feather their blonde strands
as if by magic, like a trick out of the sleight
of hand they don't care about, like the plastic
comb that sits easily in the back pocket of
their Ditto's. Like a French kiss outside the window
of algebra class in the bungalow, or getting
secret admirer red carnations on Friday
from Jessie, the king of the universe.
The flip and saddle back jeans and the ever-present
grape Lip Smacker, every sentence twirled onto
the mouth to make sparkle-words. The smooth dexterity
looking forward to an open gate for a place I never went to,
a Friday dance gymnasium with a fancy backless dresses
my parents cannot buy.
The charm of sweet conflict, snarled waves,
my Portuguese frizz waves, a divorce of emotions between what
I see in the locker and who I see far away
in the pages of Seventeen magazine, near
from the teenage experience of greatness, charity,
a catalog of friends I could never connect with.
And, the ever-present relief that damn it. I know this moment
to be as true as true can be. Like a true slow dance
with Ruben to "Baby, I love your Way."

We Count Steps, Sweep Soreness

from "Cumbia de Salvación" by Leticia Hernández-Linares

From our joints in celebration
for what is to come,
there was a quarantine of smoke
and everyone had to stay put.
There were birthdays and funerals and dinners
Out that did not happen.
Like a found philosophical
teaching lesson we missed, we find ourselves
regrouping and struggling in
a haze of our converted nonchalance.
We are masculine and passionate,
in a place on a corner near Rec Park
when we wish things were different,
and we could sing, "Let's Stay Together."
In this new world where our borders
are inner beings rotated six feet under
without witnesses. We are a split nation
and acting civil and apparent.
We are too bold to sit tight.
And, we are completely temperate,
sober and angry, as if it were 1920
and there was an unconquerable flag of soberness
throughout the America experiment.
We wish we belonged to the weight
of the great depression cast down upon
us like a cellar door, opening, in the middle of a cold
sidewalk, with ice strewn about.

My Body is a Flame

from "shame: a ghazal in pieces" by irene lara silva

And, I am ashes, turning over to extinguish
the inevitable. My civility, apparent, having
a total hold on reality, shaken to ice once again.
When will I do better at predicting what
will happen next, the muscles I need
to loosen or tense up to engage in the
next river heading water down the banks
of my life. Completely unfettered, I allow
what is to occur, unmethodical and edgy
to take over. I let it take over, fearing the other
shoe from falling out a window ten stories
above my head as I walk by,
heading straight for me, like a thought
I had, creative, wild, uncontrollable.
Like life-blood or sex. A something
Like a moment where I can see doom
happening, like a crack in the sidewalk or
a warning I know will come true.

Until Beaten, my Wings

from "Scenes in the life of a lesser angel" by Raina León

The word
blue can be a noun.
This confuses
the language
and out-softs the definition
of what it means to be
right as rain,
like can you be blue sad and the blue color
Can that exist? And
then you might not get
a handle on things.
Like, when you are confused
about what is being
said and nothing makes sense.
Cause it may be blue,
and look like someone is fixing
a fence or they are
breaking a thing, like your spirit
or who you are is in its place,
traded places.
The color is taking over.
And then you are in it
and cannot stop
the feeling-action like a strong engine
of anger stuck in the On
down-go- floor-it-now position,
like it is unstoppable
you are being slammed
down on your neck
with people standing around

and there is nothing you can do.
Death is here,
no matter what comes next.

Come Angels! Come Beasts!

from "Angels in the Sun" by Ruben Quesada

And it talked about how the younger ones
were standing
out and they were naïve but the older ones knew and this boy
standing out in the parking lot of this father Cimarron;
Starlight, Skydancer, maybe Cinnamon.
For years he would abuse and beat, making the boys suck him
And he was able to avoid
until no one said anything Even after he retired
And went to an old priests' home
Where he relaxed and sipped brandy
And talked about things.
He escaped it all.
I was trying to figure out when my older brother went there
1958. 1959. He came home ten years later,
Broken, on the couch. Crying
Before he got work at a fish cannery.
The time frame of an article about the priest
Was vague maybe the 1970's, and it was talking about
St Anthony's and Santa Barbara
Franciscan seminaries.
The name there, I mean,
If my brother was not actually touched,
he would have been aware.
Or, he noticed how certain students
Were singled out as weak or pretty.
The guy that wrote the article said
Those who stayed thru, til graduation
accepted that they had stayed through.
This was the way things were.
The priest held their responses

over their young heads, as if he owned them.
Midnight hernia exams, pressing through
the rolled sheets, thyroid massages
on their soft neck, their heads
bent over his lap for spankings
while he sweated.
The boys later described their faces as
hot and red, being shoved face-down
into his lap
as he prayed for them.
It was hard to know which was worse,
For my brother, if anything,
going though it or refusing to help
those he could have.

I Told my Friend to Rub her Lice Against my Hair

from "How I Learned to Walk" by Javier Zamora

So I could get the comb through and deal with
the nasty lotion and the sitting on a chair in front
of the low kitchen sink so my mother would
love me and fuss over my hair and touch
my chin instead of being afraid as to what would happen.
My grandma told the Yanis family on Cherry
to play with me when they had Chicken Pox ,
so I would not have to stand in line at Thrifty
Drug. Through the open screen, my mom
yelled down at my parents' bedroom, down
at the porch swing in the yard below,
with the rusty swig set from Sears,
where me and my avó waved
at her in a rag slung over her head and jaw,
cause she had the mumps.
My mom said careful. Don't breathe in,
and it won't be long until you can come
back to the house. I sealed the sugar
cubes of polio close as they melted
into my mouth when we took the 12 bus downtown
to Long Beach Pine Ave and got the shots
for everything and my avó
told me not to tell, even though I got
a special sticker and a cherry
jubilee cone at Woolworths and it
came from a square scoop, and we missed our stop
on the way home on the Blue Bus cause Margo
was tying her beige scarf up under her chin
and looking at the wrinkled McCoy's grocery bag
she had tried to fold in her lap.

Killing too Much Meat to Carry

from "Alone on the Oregon Trail" by Juan Morales

Finding so much unlawful immediate
happiness, as if it were perpetual or not committable.
It was almost and maybe, but we were
soaring above and finding ourselves hurling into
barriers below as if we could not even tunnel underground.
My god. It was awful, the unsettling time of it all,
It was so hard, being legitimate and reckless.
Like we were reasonable and trying
to be liked, tucking in the silk shirts.
We found it all so unsupportable and unlivable,
as if we were inside a Western movie set
or a doll house, and like that has never been
done before. Finding found. Life lived.
Such lawful beings thrown apart,
Like separate toys thrown in the air,
an eternal absolute, a proud religious moment
written down like a prayer for when for people,
maybe, I dunno, could have used it
when they felt whole and human.

All Unwavering Survivors

from "Chanclas, Find Our Ground" by Gloria Amescua

Unconditional and sudden,
the last of the last
stand at attention as if they care,
or at least need to show it or prove
it to the rest of us.
Remarkable for their stillness
and fury, they are outside
a long solo flight of music,
set apart, detained, locked up,
where the earth seems
large and absolute
below them.
The sky above, complete
and slowly female in gender,
surrounds those of us
who remain
like sand and dirt as if we were
there, and always.

I Made up a Story for Myself Once

from a line by José Angel Araguz

Oh, come on. It is a mirage
inside a tunnel that you sleep
through, so wild-full and degrading
that you want to be industrial
and rise up in spite of desire.
In spite of how things should
be, or the rules people lied to you
about when you were young.
It is nearly internal, the law
called the greater good, or
a world where everyone toes
the line at attention to the masses
of law and order that the rich
brag about, far away from the assembly line.
And we know. We all
know that this is not true or gracious,
and definitely not what we were born
for. Hiding under the coffee table
for the fear to go away, we settle down
and decide to think of scrambled eggs
and Pepsi in a can. Where you
close your eyes and send you
back to the safe place,
where you can say Yes and
where you most want to be.

Boys from Lisbon, a Block Away

inspired by "City Moon" by Francisco Aragón

The Portuguese say every family has a whore,
a thief, and a bully. Decades of generations and
terror, walk under the porch, the brother
who went off to be a priest, the rest of us
hiding from the fear of violence, the tree switch,
a parent chasing around the block,
others at home under tables, afraid to move.
There were so many tables and hiding inside
the circular clothing racks at Sears so no
one could find me inside my fallacy, my nest
of a fort where all I saw were pumps and silk
legs, covered in sunset or nude.
Detain, hold, intern, confine
hide, I was to lock up, be inside.
The crisp sound as hangers scratched the metal
rods while customers sorted through the dresses
and jumpers on the hangers and looked at paper tags,
clutched and opened purses, thrown down used
Kleenex, gum wrappers, the people who shifted their weight.
fighting a dark listlessness, a distant indifference
of making a final choice, to select or
leave behind, to pay for with a price tag and take safely
home for keeps.

Cool like the Río Medina Under the Trees

from a line in "Caminitos" by Carmen Tafolla

It was something he said
about being named after a children's
show, by his brother,
a fair-clipped attempt to soften
the blow of the end of being an only
child. The nuances of parenthood,
of seeking out differences in infancy,
gathering information from books and
remembering to bring back the kid
after custody time was up on the weekends,
even on Christmas even on summer holidays,
where the humidity seemed a calculated genius
conclusion that the days were longer
spent in a parked car waiting for a moment
of custody. The shortest day arrives
in December, amid a cloud of soap bubbles
and oranges stuffed with cloves,
unseasonably ripe in baskets at the entrance
to Boys Market.
We are on the way to the river,
before the axis turns on its heel and heads back
to the changing distance where
no one touches each other, not
even under the night covers. We gather
up our shawls to face a new apathy, with
masks and handkerchief creations.
Mathematicians during the Spanish Flu,
said it spread thru the population
like everything else does,
that it travels through a population, like

the wind, like gossip,
that it starts low, then peaks,
and descends in the shape of a
large curved bell. Like a rumor, the virus
transmission starts to descend as the population achieves
immunity, saturation, or death.

The Poor Kid with Something to Prove

from "American Marine" by Diego Báez

All guts and glory and tired of begging,
he is the least likely target for being up
for anything. Laying his life out on a plate.
He is the serenity prayer come to life,
the punk with no attitude,
a person ready to fight anyone, all squirrely
and alive, having nothing to lose, it is to say
that it is what he was meant to be,
a hero, to do for himself, to exist
within a life about to be spilt open
like an orange into four pieces.
He goes to the corner for something deathless
and personal, chewing gum or Papst.
No Nat Sherman's or Marlboros.
He is unchanged-strong and tight,
like a hand-rolled cigarette.
Pent up his spine a blind stranger to even
himself, his wants are almost like
a challenge for the fact that nothing
can get in his way. He is solely
glorious-rare and in the pocket moment of
be here now, and leave me when you have to,
cause, it's all right. The storm will rage
and the aftermath will still be here tomorrow,
despite what happens in the immediate now.
He is comfortable and familiar-real, a member
of the paternal sorrow, that opened up when he was born.
Ready for tenacious-guilt and the progressive-sexual
beings that lifers larger than the most miserable
steadfast men in the wilds of the grateful universe

hope for, to dream about when their eyes close
in the early morning. He is heading for
the way things are, the able-amazing vision of now.
Boys who are full of promise, marching to all
the delightful nouns he can think of in this split second
time of his own choosing. The true-larger,
needlessly-bold pathway to forever
That he is walking on.

The Sky's in the Middle of Descent

from "Dustlore No. 35" by Anthony Cody

The faithful-infinite, unspeakable silence
dwells in the house of never forgiving.
We try and we negotiate and compromise,
but--the thing is—we are always there,
possessive and dull.
The silence, it beats away your possible
senses, taking you through the descent
into comfort and sameness
until people are the most miserable
people we know, and we try to defend
ourselves as the stronghold of water and
wood as we slip away from under our feet
with no hint of the drowning.
Childlike and chaste,
we wish for the best and throw
our familiar-real
selves into the faithful-infinite sky
as we inexhaustibly
delight in our own lack of just how to cope.

Saguaros, Purple Blossoms Open in the Moonlight

from "Sierra Amnezia" by Michael Dauro

We dwindle and recant and unbind out of our
fullest local selves, always in astonishment
at what unrestrained matters we dwell on.
The handsomely loyal friend
who becomes careless and less than divine when the
sun comes up or you disagree about being sick.
During an awful moment of awfulness
when you need him the most, he fails in the light
thinking that everything is a choice you can make
of it. That we are more-corresponding people, careless
and masculine, tough as nails, and as if we will
always be this way. In command of our faculties
--as my grandmother used to say--until things went south.
We are outwardly religious and thankful,
unclothed in our naivety. As if we knew it all.
Does anyone really know what is coming next.
The purple blossom I find in early morning
near the mail box, blooming over-night. They
are ignorant of us and unified. We tooth it out together,
admiring each other in obscurity. Hoping
and setting our sights on joy. Life is much-fleeting
and everything is a dizzying phone call away,
At best. Those are the times to say, I am sorry.
At worst, life is unmanageable and ignorant.
We keep losing our footing on the utterly defiant
proper noun, a perfect, new-found and hard-won
consensual term, a form of the word Yes that
I take for No. But, we keep at it, sharing in the distant
beauty, like chewing a quiet form of affection, something we
both want badly. We are sincere, disheveled and aiming high.

There are no promises here. We take what we can get,
and make the best of the things that we are the best We take what we can get at.

Doors Flung Open

from "The Daughter" by Carmen Gimenez Smith

They slammed the family together
and the princess phone was tugged
out of the wall outlet, the heavy hall
door slung open and
slammed so hard that it broke the hinges
off the frame that had allowed the door
to swing open since 1923.
There was rage and anger known
only as foreign countries to parents
couched deeply in wanting children,
wanting the kisses, and the toddler-happy
moments of baby photos.
Who had no idea of relative delight,
In celebrating the utter defiant deception
of the delight and longings of an angry
adolescent girl at her peak of rage,
in the room where she had lost popsicles and ribbons,
throwing about cast-off Baby Tender Loves.
And, it was all about the legal, impersonal chaotic
freedom, given to her in a yellow release note
by a guidance counselor who told her
to meet him in Recreation Park.
She had all the power, an exhilarating-gutter
of unfettered easiness with her mouth,
the so-called easy welcoming gesture that
was possible as a matter of fact, enrobed in
a new delight, long gone from the blue canopy bed
the provincial chest of drawers, the days
that she left behind, as a lasting devotion
to the heart spent freedom that she felt

she was promised when she
left to be more than what she had had.

One Season, my Father Leases Land to Grow Fresno Sweet Red Onions

from "Onions" by Juan Luis Guzmán

Reading this, I cook Fresno peppers into Piri Piri sauce,
red melting the spice to the Portuguese catch-all phrase
for adding a teaspoon of red flavor into cooking.
The deception of hot, couched into sweetness
Mixed among red onions.
We see the vivid color and forget the trouble
we are going through endured in the sweet-hot flavor.
Quarantine, not so unbearable when there is beautiful.
Isolation, seclusion, set apart.
A teaming marriage of thin skin and boiling water, the garlic
at hand, ready for the waiting time between
crushing peppers and putting into a jar,
a limbo sauce no one else knows about,
I secretly add it to eggs and soup.
It is my mystery for chicken and marriage.
To be bright red is to want things to happen.
I know this and make Piri Piri, to be held
carefully, to be used later.
The nuances of honey and bitter, roll
about my tongue as I add the sauce to
our lives. In disbelief, we cannot imagine
how much like flavors, the home becomes.
like a disturbance. Like crudeness. Like candor.
Food is what we are about and this is the
chaos as we live inside the safety net.

Green was the Silence

from a line by Pablo Neruda

It changes meaning like water,
as a living being, like unfettered civility,
a sunny breezeful summer ahead.
The start of June, it is altogether
Stifling, and as if things would never be straight
again we feel as if we had promised to be
dark and mortal, soon, like strangers
from the past we promised to be each other's
solid memory. We have shortness of breath
and a pounding inside the lungs.
We cannot remember a time when we were able
to sleep before when we were former and usual
vivid beings who existed in the city of Los Angeles,
drifting through rivers of errands and emeralds,
as if nothing had happened. We are
lost now. As if we had been careless. Dropped out.
like music not written down but whistled and hummed
and played under strange circumstances.
Like a stranger with a guitar at a party.
It is nearly June, near the longest day of the year,
as Jordan comments in *The Great Gatsby*, a seasonal marker
complete with a sign that says, "We're done now."
And we are together and alone and about to
get reckless and cruel, but yet this time it will
be different. This year, belonging to the entangled
world that has been ripped apart.
We are limited by so many things since
the quarantine, absolute touch and hunger
and it all goes to show us that nothing
is visible or at hand any more.

We are a perfect example of ration
and virtue, essentially savage and, yet--in a new sense--
we are blindly controllable. We feel alternately
safe and in danger, every moment altered,
with no telling which statement above is truer.
We are reckless-absolute and sexual-reasonable
full of home-shocked martyrdom and wary of being
present for what is about to come. We pretend
to be on holiday and take
out the board games, self-full of pride and fear,
notching achievements with false pride:
your charm, my conflict—our 24 hour conversations
lack a richness of reality,
embodied with a generous sadness.

More Than us, but Less than Wind

from a line by Carmen Giménez Smith

The times when I cannot meet
you halfway, we struggle
you know how to say this word,
migration, immigration, destiny.
The scattering of people, traveling
away from where they were born,
from war, violence, famine, poverty,
disease. The diaspora stretches out
like a fishing net, across the Mexico
Border and California, Texas, Arizona.
Dragging culture across grassy fields,
dragging language around like a knapsack,
empting familiar phrases as if they were bread
crumbs along the way. How much can we carry?
What do we leave or stay. How much of ourselves
do we remain within our leaving hearts,
the gateway to our lives, our rabbit's foot,
the pelt worn down to bone and dried blood
that we finger in our nearly closed fist
when we are scared.

Darkness we are Having

from a line by Jane Kenyon

Then, right is used as a verb,
a signpost of what we are supposed to
suppress and keep quiet about as if we
never had the whole world inside our
puerperal vision. Rights are used to change
the subject in a discussion or discourse,
they used to mean a solution to someone who
is out of line, as if an interjection, like, Oh Dear
or Not me is an excuse for the abrupt remark
out of place, a remark of strong emotions.
Like a long sentence that trails off, filled with
the dense flavor of putting up with orders spoken
to us, as if it would always be this way, the way
that it is now. As if we had always been this way.
We keep trying to learn when to stuff it. When to focus
on the heat inside the bones, their marrow beat.
For instance, we count, for a moment, the pause
when it is time to move, to speak. When the word
right is used as a verb, we correct, we are faced
with righting all the wrongs of a given afternoon,
swallowing the list of needs to be less than
impossible, as as if any war will be impossible
like us, including the war inside our bodies
telling us to move or stretch our atrophied
muscles, parched from bouts of dehydration.
The communal world of being female is fluid.
We bathe in we speak and we are often
the difference between words. Opinions
righted as if they were a flipped vehicle
stranded on a middle highway strip, stuck,

broken, bent over as if to say, Oh, that tow truck
righted the green Buick when he wind died down.
Affecting the end result is to return to normal.
We sit on our hands, the state of being
used like action verbs, We run, we attack
We attach, sometimes splitting open the old usage of
slang terms, what words are meant to mean:
is, was, to be. Are we in a state of being half.
Moreover, needing to shut up and curl into
that shape who complies inside the full moon
and shines clear the definitions of justice, law, reason.
We are, after all, filled with a lack of agitation, an immigrant
disturbance. Peaceful talk they say, at random
and set into place, between the almost given, neatly
as if no one noticed us there, as if that is the darkness
that we are having, the state of being serene.

Wet was the Light

from a line by Pablo Neruda

Wet was the light as we saw it
through a threadbare lens
of what we call time or that period
of waiting between what will happen
next and what we regret having happened,
the hard-bad opposite of a world hunch or an omen,
the silent-low sense of doom to come,
a spirit arising in the country we
call home, the desire for isolation,
desperately to be different, the
unexplored nonsense of late.
This is the air in the pastel room when we
are enclosed and locked up by
an intense wondering and fear
of comfort fear of letting our guard
down and forgetting to protect ourselves
from nearly everything we can imagine,
even the scrape of skin upon
our hands, the whispered hello
of a neighbor or a child playing in the creek
below the yard where there are dirt
banks instead of lawn. We are who
we choose to become, are becoming
or perhaps we mean we are who we
are sentenced to be, a corona crown
of in the if and now and meant for always
that time is a path to follow, as we near the
day of the year when June rises
her longest glance of a day and tells us
it is all right to enter.

Endnotes

The poetry in *Quarantine Highway* was written during early and mid-pandemic months, a number of pieces were created as part of a 30 by 30 writing challenge, organized by Juan Morales for CantoMundo fellows (past and present), and other poems were influenced by readings or themes initiated by books and gatherings via Zoom, during an isolated time where poetry once again drew us close, reunited our spirits and held our souls safely within our own and each other's isolation.

José Tolentino Mendonça, Emily Perez, Gerardo Pacheco, Rosebud Ben-Oni, Alexis Smithers, Inês Fonseca Santos, Nuno Júdice, Cynthia Cruz, Kim Göransson, Rusty Morrison, Marilyn Kallet, Carl Marcum, Amy Sayre Baptista, Deborah Paredez, Norma Cantu, Carlo Matos, Celeste Guzmán Mendoza, Ángel García, Eduardo C. Corral, Carolina Ebeid, Diana Marie Delgado, Sheryl Luna, Laurie Ann Guerrero, Luivette Resto, Leticia Hernández-Linares, Ire'ne Lara Silva, Raina León, Robert Manaster, Jean Colonomos, Ruben Quesada, Javier Zamora, Juan Morales, Elizabeth Acevedo, Gloria Amescua, José Angel Araguz, David Campos, PaulA Neves, Francisco Aragón, Carmen Tafolla, Diego Báez, Anthony Cody, Michael Dauro, Carmen Gimenez Smith, Pablo Neruda, and Juan Luis Guzmán.

About the Author

Millicent Borges Accardi, an NEA fellow, is a Portuguese-American writer. She has three poetry collections. Among her awards are fellowships from the National Endowment for the Arts, California Arts Council, CantoMundo, Fulbright, Foundation for Contemporary Arts NYC (Covid grant), Creative Capacity, Fundação Luso-Americana, and Barbara Deming Foundation, "Money for Women." She lives in the hippie-arts community of Topanga, CA where she curates Kale Soup for the Soul and co-curates Loose Lips poetry readings.

CPSIA information can be obtained
at www.ICGtesting.com
Printed in the USA
JSHW031916281022
32058JS00002B/44